DOMINOES AND SOLITAIRE.

By "BERKELEY."

CONTENTS.

DOMINOES.

INTRODUCTION.

THE game of Dominoes is by many people looked upon as a childish amusement, and wholly unworthy of the attention of lovers of games; but those who are better acquainted with the niceties of the "Draw game," and the odd situations often produced by the Matadore game, are quite of another opinion, and are altogether convinced that dominoes ranks as equal, if not as superior, to many of the card games highly spoken of, much played, and greatly appreciated by those who consider themselves judges of such matters.

Dominoes, there is very little doubt, is not a mere game of chance, as any ordinary player would soon find out to his cost were he to try conclusions with an "old domino hand." Something more than good cards is required to achieve victory; skill founded on accurate calculation, ready observation, and rapid deduction from such observation, and in addition good temper, are some of the capabilities necessary for playing the game well.

In a humble way it resembles whist in two or three particulars. A long suit, *i.e.*, several cards of the same denomination, such as six-one, six-three, six-four, six-five, is the backbone of a good hand. The long suit should be played as soon as possible, and when established will enable a player to block his adversary and win, or at any rate will aid the holder thereof in averting a disastrous defeat. Again, the quick observation, and the light thrown upon what the adversary holds, by what he plays, and by what he refrains from playing, have also their analogy in whist.

Here, as in whist, a skilful player will occasionally play "false cards," that is, will depart from the accepted rules of play, in order to deceive, it may be, a wily adversary; but before a player can venture to try such artifices he ought to be thoroughly conversant with the tactics of the game, as otherwise he will often defeat himself by the very means which he fondly believes will prevent his adversary from doing so. Even an average player is able to gain some insight into an adversary's hand if he carefully note his play; and by calculating a few moves ahead, may either block the game or keep it open, according to the exigencies of the moment.

This game, of which there are many variations, good, bad, and indifferent, fourteen of which we are about to describe in the following pages, is placed by Hoyle, and very properly so, among mixed games of chance and skill.

The proportions of each differ greatly according to the kind of game played. From a purely scientific standpoint it might be only necessary to describe two, or at most three, kinds; but we have reason to hope that our readers will belong to many classes, some requiring an amusing game to while away a weary hour, some wishing to gamble in a mild way with a party of congenial spirits, while others may look at games in a more serious light, and desire to be shown the most scientific modes of playing this varied and highly interesting game.

We will first give general rules applicable for the most part to all the variations; then a description of each variety, more or less in detail, according to their merit in our eyes; and finally treat the Draw and Matadore games as fully as the space allotted to this subject will permit.

The two varieties above mentioned are in our opinion far ahead of all the others, quite as much as Rubicon piquet is superior to the English variety, chess to draughts, or we might even venture to add, as whist is to nap or loo.

DESCRIPTION OF THE GAME.

Dominoes is played by two or more persons (according o the variation chosen) with twenty-eight pieces—technically styled "cards"—of oblong shape, composed of ivory or bone, plain at the back, but on the face divided by a black line across the middle into two equal squares, each square being indented with spots or left blank, as shown in the diagram on page 6.

There are also domino sets, published in neat little boxes, made of cardboard. These, however, are not so handy as the old-fashioned dominoes, although in one variety, namely Domino loo, they are a great convenience.

The pieces, twenty-eight in number, are—double-blank ; one-blank, double-one ; two-blank, two-one, double-two ; three-blank, three-one, three-two, double-three ; four-blank, four-one, four-two, four-three, double-four ; five-blank, five-one, five-two, five-three, five-four, double-five ; six-blank, six-one, six-two, six-three, six-four, six-five, and double-six. They will all be found in the diagram on page 6.

Sometimes sets ranging up to double-nines and double-twelves respectively are used, but the pack shown in the diagram is the one generally played with, especially in the games meant for two players, the higher sets being only used in the round games.

Although many of the hints suggested in the following pages will apply to games played with the higher sets, yet all the games which are treated at any length are played with twenty-eight cards, the highest of which is the double-six.

It may not be out of place to mention at once that the "double-twelve" set contains ninety-one dominoes, and their aggregate number of pips is 1,092, *i.e.*—they average twelve pips on each.

"Double-nine" set contains fifty-five dominoes, and their aggregate number of pips is 495, and average nine pips each.

These details are of little practical value in the higher sets, as a player will have to be guided by his cards whether it is advisable to block the game or leave it open.

If a player holds a light hand, and an equal or less number of dominoes than his opponent or opponents, he should block, and not otherwise. If his cards average five or less, he has a light hand; and if six or more, he has a heavy hand.

In the "double-six" set, this point, on the other hand, is one of considerable importance, at least to those who desire to play the game on scientific principles.

42	21	30	15	20	10	12	6	6	3	2	1	.	.

168 pips in all.

It will be seen by the above diagram that the "double-six " set consists of twenty-eight dominoes, whose aggregate number of pips is 168, consequently each domino averages six.

Again, each suit contains seven dominoes, as will be evident in the case of the six and blank suits; and as regards the others, suppose you want to see the "two" suit, you will have to look along the third horizontal column, and on coming to the end of it you carry your eye down the perpendicular column, which joins the end of the third horizontal column.

One of the chief difficulties in estimating quickly the number of pips already played is that the suits intermingle.

The six	suit contains	sixty-three	pips.
The five	,,	,,	fifty-six	,,
The four	,,	,,	forty-nine	,,
The three	,,	,,	forty-two	,,
The two	,,	,,	thirty-five	,,
The one	,,	,,	twenty-eight	,,
The blank	,,	,,	twenty-one	,,

When we treat of the tactics of the Draw game, this subject will be gone into more in detail (page 28).

Having now described the implements of warfare, we will proceed at once to describe how they are to be used.

The cards should first of all be turned with their faces downwards, and shuffled with a slight circular motion of the hands. Then the question as to who is entitled to the lead should be determined.

There are various ways of doing this in vogue among domino players.

Drawing for the Lead.

The first and simplest method is that each player draws a card from the pack after it has been well shuffled, and he who draws the lowest double wins the lead; in default of a double being drawn, the holder of the card bearing the least number of pips wins "the down." If there are more than two players, this draw will also decide seats and the sequence of the lead in the remaining hands of that game. The person who draws the second lowest card sits to the leader's left hand, and has the lead in the second hand; and the holder of the third lowest sits next, and has the lead in the third hand, and so on.

The lead, however, is cut for afresh after every game.

The second method is, that one player pushes two dominoes to his adversary; the opponent chooses one, and if it is the lower, he leads,—if not, he plays second.

The third method is one very prevalent among French players; namely, that he who is dealt the highest double, or, in case of there being no double dealt, the heaviest card, has the lead. The double-six is called for first; if absent, the double-five, and so on. The holder of the highest card has to lead with it.

This method in our opinion is cumbrous, lengthy, and has the great disadvantage of compelling a player to make a false and sometimes even a most disadvantageous lead.

The plan to be recommended is the first one given, but it is not a matter of any very great importance, and players can follow their own inclination.

The Deal.

The lead being determined, and the cards re-shuffled, each player takes a certain number of dominoes, varying according to the game chosen, which constitute his hand. This is termed the deal.

The cards not dealt form the " stock " or "reserve." The " stock " is sometimes drawn from after the cards are dealt, and we shall use the word in this sense.

When the cards remaining over after the deal are left untouched, as in the Block and such-like games, we shall call such cards " the reserve."

Let it be clearly understood, however, that when the " stock " is drawn from, on no account is it permissible for either or any player to completely exhaust it, as two cards must always remain in it, unseen by any player.

The Mode of Play.

The cards having been dealt, are either ranged upright in a line on the table, or are held in the palm of the hand, with their faces so arranged as not to be seen by the adversary. The leader has to "pose," *i.e.*, he has to play any card he may choose from his hand, placing it face upwards on the table. The next player follows in the same way, and the rest follow in turn. Each player, however, is bound by this restriction, that he must follow suit, *i.e.*, must match the number of pips or blank shown on one or other of the ends of the dominoes already "posed."

Having chosen which end, he places his domino with that end adjacent to the corresponding number on the domino already on the table.

Suppose A plays five-two to a five-six " posed," thus—

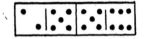

he must place the two fives together, as shown above.

The next to play must now "pose" a card containing one of the numbers at either open end. In the diagram above, he would have to play either a six or a two.

Below is given a game in progress, which will point out to the reader the best method of placing the doubles, and also the way to obviate a long straight row of cards.

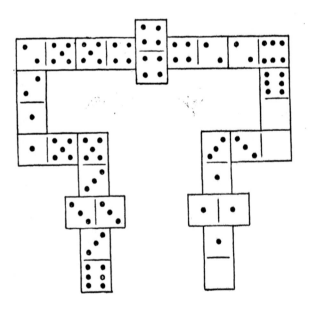

If the second player be unable to match, he has either to pass, saying "go," when the next player has similarly to play, or pass, or the second player has to "draw," *i.e.*, take one or more cards from the "stock," according to the kind of game being played.

In the Draw games, two dominoes at least must be left in the "stock," and when a player has exhausted the "stock" to this extent, and is still unable to match, he must "pass." To "pass" is only to forfeit the turn, and does not preclude the player from playing the next time his turn comes round.

Each player is bound to pose, if able.

In this manner the game is continued, until one player has played out all the cards in his hand, when he calls "domino," or until the game becomes so blocked that neither of the players can match or draw.

When any player calls "domino," the hand or game is over.

Scoring.

This is arranged in many different ways. Sometimes each hand constitutes a game in itself; and when this is so, the player who makes "domino" wins. If there is a "block," the cards in each hand are exposed on the table, and the player who holds the smallest number of pips wins. In case of equality of pips, the smallest number of dominoes is considered a win.

More commonly, however, games are played a hundred up. In this case, a series of hands is played, the lead being taken alternately by the players. If there are more than two players, the lead passes round the table to the left.

Any variations beyond these two will be noticed under the respective games in which they occur.

Each player should keep his own score, either on paper or by means of a domino marker.

THE VARIOUS GAMES.

THESE can be conveniently arranged under three heads :—

    I. The Block game and its varieties.

    II. The Draw game and its variety the Matadore.

    III. Miscellaneous games.

Of the Block, or English game, there are many varieties, the best-known of them being All Fives or Muggins, All Threes, Domino Whist, the Four game, Sebastopol, Cyprus, Tiddle-a-wink, and Domino Pool.

THE BLOCK GAME.

THIS is the most ordinary form of dominoes for two players ; it is also called "the English game," or "Double Sixes."

The cards are shuffled, and the lead drawn for, as already described. Each player takes seven dominoes at random. Fourteen dominoes will thus be disposed of; the remaining fourteen are left face downwards on the table, and form the "reserve."

The winner of the first pose now puts down a card on the table, and the game proceeds in the usual manner.

The game is won by the player who makes "domino," or, if the game is blocked, by the one whose cards show the lesser number of pips.

If the game, however, consists of a hundred, or some

other fixed number, the maker of "domino" scores all the pips on his adversary's cards; or if there is a "block," the holder of the lesser number of pips scores in one of three ways, as may be agreed upon :—

(1) Either the number of pips held by both players added together;
(2) Or the number held by his adversary;
(3) Or the difference between his own and adversary's pips.

The first of these is recommended, as it renders the game more interesting, and does away with indiscriminate blocking.

The cards are then re-shuffled, and a fresh hand is made.

The Tactics of the Game.

1. Examine your hand carefully on taking it up, note your long suit, and bear in mind that the object of this game is twofold—to get rid of your own dominoes as soon as possible, and to prevent your adversary from getting rid of his.

2. Play therefore those bearing a number most frequently found in your hand—in other words, your strong suit.

3. Note that three of a suit is strong, as it is highly improbable your adversary holds four of that suit, or even three. The larger the number of any suit held in your hand, the greater are the chances that none or few of the same suit will be among your adversary's cards.

4. If it is indifferent which of two cards you play, choose the one that bears the larger number of pips, in order to hold as few pips as possible when you have to count.

5. Retain doubles in hand as little as possible, because they are twice as difficult to place as ordinary cards. But if you hold several doubles, wait until your opponent gives you a chance of playing them, in preference to making opportunities for yourself; otherwise an experienced player will understand your drift, and block your double.

6. If you hold a double, and two or three others of one suit, it is your strong suit; and if leader, you should pose the double; but if not, place your strong suit at both ends, it possible. If you succeed in placing it only at one end, and you are blocked at the other, play your double, in hopes your adversary's next move may open the blocked end.

7. If there is a number at one end of the game which belongs to your strong suit, or which your opponent evidently shirks, follow him at his end, as the chances are that he cannot go at the other, which you may keep open for yourself, until you are unable to play at his end.

8. When it is at your option whether to block the game or not, you must be guided by your adversary's previous play, as to whether his hand is light or heavy, and decide accordingly. In absence of any indications, base your calculation on the consideration that the average number of pips on all the dominoes is six; and thus if those played out and those in your own hand average less than six, and your adversary has an equal or greater number of cards than you have, it is advisable to block.

9. At the commencement of the game, a light varied hand, such as six-two, five-three, four-one, four-blank, three-two, two-blank, one-blank, is an excellent one. In the first place it is nine pips below the average, is varied, and contains a long suit—namely, twos. Varied hands are even to be preferred to a long suit, in that you may never have

the opportunity of playing a long suit to advantage, whereas a mixed hand will enable you to keep both ends of the game open to yourself, at any rate for a few moves. Of course, on the other hand, several heavy doubles would be a very bad hand.

10. When second player, endeavour to mislead your adversary by playing at each end indifferently. This is often more advantageous than playing to his last domino.

11. If one end is blocked to you, but open to your opponent, try to play one of your long suit, with a view to forcing him to play at the end blocked to you, thereby shutting it against his strong suit.

12. It by no means necessarily follows that because a hand is heavy it must lose. Provided it be varied, it may succeed as well as a light hand, as far as winning the hand is concerned, but it labours under the disadvantage that if it loses it does so heavily, whereas if it wins, its gains are small.

13. Bring both ends as often as possible to the number of your strong suit, as such play will either block your opponent or force cards of that suit out of his hand.

14. If you hold a heavy hand, prevent your adversary from blocking the game, play your heaviest first, and keep both ends open to yourself.

15. Use your judgment freely, and do not hesitate at times to play an eccentric game, which will often prove efficacious in deceiving your adversary, especially if as a general rule you adhere to the correct game.

16. Draw as many inferences as you can from your antagonist's play, and allow him as little insight into your hand as possible.

ALL FIVES, OR MUGGINS.

THIS game, which is very popular in some circles, derives
its name from the principal object to be aimed at in the
game.   It is excellent practice for quick counting, and
success in it depends more on skill than on luck.   Two,
three, or four players may at one time take part in the game.
Each takes an equal number of dominoes, always providing
that at least two cards remain as a reserve, and that no
player has more than seven.   Five, however, is the best
number for each player.

Cards are shuffled, and pose drawn for in the usual way.
The object of the game is to play so that the aggregate
number of pips at the opposite ends of the game should
number 5, 10, 15, or 20.   All double dominoes must be
placed transversely, a rule which, though usual in most
games, is compulsory only in this and kindred ones.

If the leader can play six-four, double-five, five-blank, or
three-two, he scores two or one, as the case may be.

In the subsequent play, if a card is played that makes the
total number of pips at both ends of the game five, ten,
fifteen, or twenty, the player scores one for five, two for ten,
three for fifteen, and four for twenty.

The game may be fixed at any reasonable number, but
thirty-one makes it about equal in length to a hundred up
in the Block game.   Some low number, such as ten or
fifteen, renders it "short, sharp, and decisive," and consequently more exciting.   In order to make our meaning
clearer, we will give a short illustration.

Suppose A leads double-five and scores two.   This is of
course his best lead, as it scores two, and is an effectual
block to B scoring next time unless he plays five-blank,

which also scores two. Let B play five-six, making sixteen at the two ends, *viz.* six at one and ten at the other. Should A play five-four to the double-five end, he again scores two, as the two numbers shown at each end will be six and four, making ten.

The game proceeds in this manner until either one player calls " domino," or the game is blocked.

Four is the highest score possible at any one pose, and happens when there is a double-six at one end and double-four at the other.

Three points can be made by double-five at one end and a five at the other, or double-six at one end and three at the other.

A scoring card must be declared when played, or in default the score is lost.

At the end of the game the pips of those cards that cannot be played are added up and the number of times five is contained in the multiple of five, which is nearest to the number of pips in the adversary's hand (or in case of more than two players of the adversary's hand that shows most pips), is added to the score of the player who holds the smaller or smallest number of pips, or to the player who makes domino.

For example, A holds fewer pips than B, whose hand contains twenty-seven pips, A scores five, whereas if B held twenty-eight pips A would score six, since thirty, or six times five, is the multiple nearest to twenty-eight.

In some circles five is counted to the player who makes five at both ends, ten for ten, and so on ; this makes very little difference, only the number played for ought to be proportionately increased.

Tactics of the Game.

The next best thing to making fives yourself is to prevent your adversary doing so ; and when you purposely give your opponent the opportunity of making a point, it should be only in order to make two or three points yourself.

Suppose there is four at one end of the game, you would be justified in putting a three at the other, although you had not in your hand the three-one, if you held the six-one, as then you could let him score one in order to score two yourself. On the other hand, if you did not hold the double-three yourself, you would not be justified in making the opposite end to the four, a three, as should the double-three be held by your adversary, he would score two and you could only score a like number, and that only if you had the three-six.

When a skilful antagonist fails to avail himself of a good opening for playing a certain card, you may safely assume he does not hold it, and consequently you know one card at least in the " reserve."

Any indication of the position of certain cards, such as the instance just mentioned, should be stored up in the memory, and be turned to account when occasion offers.

If you hold three-two, always lead off with it; it is the only card in the whole pack which the adversary cannot score from. If you must play one of two dominoes, either of which, you fear, may be useful to the opponent, of course of two evils choose the less. Refresh your memory occasionally by taking a survey of the cards played, remember your adversary's strong suit, the cards he might have scored with, but did not ; and, in fact, draw as many inferences as possible from your opponent's play, but be at all times wary of risking a game upon such inferences, as he may have been purposely deceiving you. To understand your adversary's hand is most essential, both to guide you in what suits to avoid, and also to know when to block the game (see page 6).

There is also a variation of All Fives, in which a player must play each time his turn comes round, if able to match. If unable he draws, and continues to draw until he can match, when he must pose.

When four play each player is allowed to draw once only.

ALL THREES

Is only another version of the last game, and is similarly played, the only difference being that three and its multiples score in the place of five and its multiples. The opportunity of scoring is more frequent than in all-fives, and it therefore requires even closer attention on the part of the players than that game does.

For the same reason it is advisable to make the game consist of a greater number of points than that chosen in All Fives—fifty is to be recommended.

Three, six, nine, twelve, fifteen, and eighteen are the scoring numbers, and count one, two, three, four, five, and six respectively.

The highest score, namely eighteen, results from a double-six at one end and double-three or a six at the other.

In all other respects this game so resembles the preceding one that any further notice of it would be mere repetition.

DOMINO WHIST.

THIS game is played by four persons, two being partners against the other two, and the play proceeding as at whist. All the twenty-eight cards are sometimes dealt, but the game is rendered far more interesting if each player takes six cards, four remaining in the "reserve." The cards are shuffled, and the lead in the first hand drawn for, as already described.

If partners are drawn for, the two who draw the dominoes with the smallest number of pips play together.

After the "pose" the play goes round from left to right; but if any player is unable to match either end of the game, he calls "go," and forfeits his turn, and the next player in order proceeds.

The method of scoring may be arranged to suit the fancy of the players, but the best plan is for the pair who hold the smaller number of pips to score the aggregate number of pips held by their adversaries.

Each player should pay particular attention to the fall of the cards in order to baffle the adversary and help his partner. Heavy cards should be got rid of as soon as possible, unless by their means you play into your adversary's suit. If it is your lead, and you have a good hand, you must try to win with it, regardless of your partner's position. So, on the other hand, if it is your partner's "down" or "pose," and you have a bad hand, you must be content to sacrifice your hand to help him.

You should play your strong suit as often as possible in order to inform your partner. Your partner, in his turn, will either show you his suit or aid you in establishing yours, according as he is strong or weak.

It should be your endeavour to discover what cards are in the reserve, and also whether your partner's hand is heavy or light, in order to guide you whether to play for a block or to keep the game open.

It is to be remembered it is nine to two against any particular card, say the double-six or double-five, being in the " reserve," and eight to three against any particular card being in any named player's hand at the commencement of the game.

THE FOUR GAME.

THIS is simplicity itself, and is, as its name implies, intended for four players. All the twenty-eight cards are equally distributed among the players, and there is no " reserve."

The shuffling, determination of lead, and mode of play are the same as in the Block game, with the solitary exception, that instead of playing one card in a turn, a player in this variation is allowed to play as many as he can, provided all the cards played are in sequence, and can be posed at one or other of the ends of the game. Suppose a player held four-two, two-five, five-blank, double-blank, double-six, six-five, and double-five, provided the ends of the game showed a four and a six, he would be able to run out in one turn and win the game, by playing the first four of his cards at the four end, and the last three at the other.

When a block occurs before any player is able to make domino, the holder of the smallest number of pips wins.

As regards the scoring, it may be left to agreement among the players; sometimes the winner of each hand draws a certain stake from the other three, or a certain number is named for game, which may take several hands to complete.

Instruction is scarcely necessary ; mere quickness to recognise what cards will follow each other, is the great requisite for playing the game well. Cards not in sequence with the rest of your hand should be got rid of as speedily as may be.

The tactics of the game would vary considerably with each method of scoring. If merely to win the hand is your object, play the cards not in sequence first, especially if you surmise they will be disagreeable to the next antagonist. If, on the other hand, it is desirable to have as few pips as possible at the conclusion of the hand, make as long a run as you can, whenever your turn comes round.

SEBASTOPOL

Is one of the fancy variations of the Block game, in which four players can join, each taking seven dominoes, and leaving no reserve. The holder of the " double-six " is entitled to the " pose," and is obliged to play that card.

In the first round each player must play a six or call "go," and pass. In addition to playing to each end of the six, it is necessary to play to each side of it as well, when the game takes the form of a cross.

When the cross is formed, there will be four ends at which it is possible to play, and any of the arms of the cross may be continued irrespective of the condition of the others. This, of course, complicates the game to a certain extent, and renders it necessary to vary the play slightly, but many of the maxims already given will be found to hold good for this game.

For a large party this makes a very good round game, if played with "double-nine set." There are fifty-five dominoes in this pack, and they should be divided equally among the players, and the dominoes remaining over form the " reserve."

If there are ten players, each should take five ; if nine or eight, each should take six ; and if seven, each should take seven.

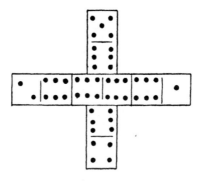

The double-nine, or highest double out, forms the centre of the cross, and entitles its possessor to the lead.

The player who makes domino, or, in case of a block, the one who holds cards with the smallest number of pips, wins.

CYPRUS.

THIS is another of the fancy variations of the Block game. It is requisite that at least a " double-nine set " be used. Four or more players can join, as in Sebastopol, and the rules are the same as in that game, with the solitary exception of the dominoes being played in the form of a star, instead of a cross.

The highest domino dealt, having been led, the succeeding players match it at each end, then at each side, and then
between these lines, as in the following diagram.

During the first round each player must match the "pose,"

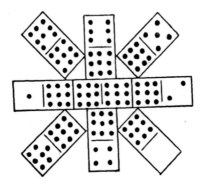

or the follow passes. It is not, however, necessary, either in
this game or in Sebastopol, that the cross or star should be
completed before the other lines are commenced, as one or
more of the suit first " posed " may remain in the reserve.

TIDDLE-A-WINK.

THIS is another of the round games at dominoes ; if it does
not give much scope for science, yet it often creates a good
deal of sport and amusement, especially if played by a merry
party.

The number of cards dealt to each player must be regu-
lated by the number of those who wish to play. If the
" double-sixes " are used, with six players, four dominoes
may be dealt to each ; with seven or eight players, three

dominoes to each. If more than eight play, the "double-nines" will be required, as at least four cards should be left in the reserve.

When the cards have been dealt, the double-six or double-nine, as the case may be, is called for; if undealt, the next highest double, and so on; the holder of the highest double has the lead, and must "pose" it, the others playing in turn in the usual way. When a player poses a "double," whether at the beginning, or at any other part of the game, he is entitled to play another card at once, provided he is able to match, if not, he cries "go," and passes.

The player who first runs out, *i.e.*, makes domino, calls out tiddle-a-wink, and wins the game.

In all other respects this game resembles the Block game.

DOMINO-POOL.

THIS game can be played by three or more players, either all against all, or as partners. The division of the cards depends on the number playing : if three play, each should take seven cards; if four, five cards each; if five, four cards each; if more, the "double-nines" will have to be used; then with six players, each should take seven; with seven players, six cards each; with eight or nine, five cards each. This leaves about a quarter of the pack as the reserve, which will be found a convenient number.

Shuffling and drawing for lead and places are decided in the usual manner. The players now take as many cards as are recommended above, and the leader "poses" a card; the player to the leader's left is obliged to match; if unable, he passes, and so on all round the table.

The game continues in this manner, until one player makes " domino," or the game is blocked.

When either of these events occurs, the score of each player is put on a piece of paper, and the cards are re-shuffled, and a new hand commenced, the eldest hand in the previous game leading, and so on, until the end of the game.

The pool is formed as at the Billiard game, from which the idea is taken, by contributions from the players.

When any player scores a hundred points (or any number agreed upon), he has lost his lives, but is at liberty to "star," *i.e.*, pay another contribution to the pool, and come into the game with a score against him equal to that of the player who has the highest score. No player is compelled to star, nor can he star more than once, but every player may star except the last two left in, who divide the pool, or play the game out, as agreed upon before the commencement of the game.

The tactics of this game resemble to a very great extent those of the Block game, only there is not so much scope for science. It is quite allowable, in the event of one player getting very far ahead, for the others to combine against him. Such combinations, however, must not be openly declared, but should naturally result as a matter of principle. On the other hand, the player who is ahead should concentrate his attention on frustrating the opponent who is nearest to him in score, as most danger is to be feared from him.

It is of very little use for one player to attempt to stop the progress of the player in the leading position, unless the other players join with him in doing so ; if they do not, he had better play his own game, because even if he attained his object, it might be at considerable personal loss.

If you find that you and one of your opponents hold

nearly all of one particular suit, combine with him in blocking the others. In playing thus, you are merely acting in your own interest.

If you hold one or two doubles, together with another card of each suit, get rid of the doubles first ; but if you hold a double and three or four of the same suit, retain your double, as you will, by your own hand, be able to bring it in later in the game.

If you are without one or more suits, play your heavy dominoes as quickly as possible ; in fact, play a defensive game.

If you have the "pose," you should lead a heavy card, unless leading your strong suit gives you a better chance of success.

With a heavy hand, containing several doubles, you should play a safe game, and endeavour to sustain as little loss as possible under the circumstances.

When there are only three players left in, say A, B, C ; A is a long way ahead, and C has starred, B should prolong the game as long as possible, and equalise A's and C's score, as he himself has always the chance of "starring," should it be worth his while.

When two players are a long way in advance of the rest, the latter should avoid embarrassing each other in their combinations against the leaders. It is advisable that the joint attack should be concentrated on one of the leaders, as it will then be more effectual.

Of course we might extend these remarks to a greater length, as there are many other points worthy of notice, but we hope we have written enough to enable our readers to play this game fairly well, and we must leave other points to their unaided judgment.

There are several variations to this game, one of which is

that a player, when he plays a double, is allowed to pose a second domino. This we do not recommend.

In scoring also, it is sometimes arranged as follows : Suppose the game is 100 up, then each player scores as many pips as he has remaining in his hand, when play ceases. The one who first scores a hundred loses points to each of the others, according to the difference in their scores. For instance, A, B, C, D play and C has 100, A 50, B 80, and D 98. Then C loses 50 points to A, 20 to B, and 2 to D. The method we have adopted seems, however, to be in accordance with the name of the game, and " starring " makes it different from the other round games of Dominoes.

THE DRAW GAME.

THIS game, like the ordinary English one, is played with twenty-eight dominoes, ranging from double-six to double-blank.

The shuffling and drawing for lead should be as usual, but as this game is of French origin the lead is in many circles decided as described in the third method (see page 8).

The dominoes are again shuffled, and each player takes seven dominoes. Sometimes six is the number agreed upon, but we decidedly advise the former number being adopted.

The player who has the right to commence poses a card, and the second player plays as directed on page 9, but previous to playing he is allowed to draw from the " stock " as many cards as he likes, provided he leaves at least two cards. Thus the game proceeds, each player being allowed to draw from the " stock " when his turn comes round, until one or other of the players cannot "go," when he is *obliged* to draw from the stock, until he is able to match or until the stock is exhausted, *i.e.*, has only two cards remaining in it. If still unable to match, he must pass.

When neither player can match, it is a block.

If a player makes domino, he scores the pips which are shown on the cards in his adversary's hand. If the game has terminated in a block, the holder of the smaller number of pips wins, and is entitled to count the pips in his adversary's hand as well as his own.

But should the pips in each hand prove exactly equal, the holder of the fewer dominoes is considered the winner, and counts the pips in both hands. · For instance, if A has twenty pips on four dominoes, and B twenty pips on five dominoes, A counts forty and B nothing.

The game consists of 100 points or any smaller number agreed upon.

In this and the Matadore game so much depends on holding the lesser number of pips, and on blocking the game exactly at the right moment, that we consider it a subject which must be gone into as deeply as the space at our disposal will permit. Consequently, before commencing the general tactics of the game we will give—

TABLES OF AVERAGES.

TABLE No. 1.

When all the—	The unplayed dominoes average—		
Sixes are out	5	Fifteen pips on every 3 cards.	
Fives ,,	$5\frac{1}{3}$	Sixteen ,, ,,
Fours ,,	$5\frac{2}{3}$	Seventeen ,, ,,
Threes ,,	6	Eighteen ,, ,,
Twos ,,	$6\frac{1}{3}$	Nineteen ,, ,,
Ones ,,	$6\frac{2}{3}$	Twenty ,, ,,
Blanks ,,	7	Twenty-one ,, ,,

TABLE No. 2.

When all the—   The unplayed dominoes average—

Sixes and fives are out		4	Twenty on every 5 cards.
,,	fours ,,	4⅖	Twenty-two	,,
,,	threes ,,	4⅘	Twenty-four	,,
,,	twos ,,	5⅕	Twenty-six	,,
,,	ones ,,	5⅗	Twenty-eight	,,
,,	blanks ,,	6	Thirty	,,

TABLE No. 3.

When all the—   The unplayed dominoes average—

Fives and fours are out		4⅘	Twenty-four pips on every 5 cards.
,,	threes ,,	5⅕	Twenty-six	,,	,,
,,	twos ,,	5⅗	Twenty-eight	,,	,,
,,	ones ,,	6	Thirty	,,	,,
,,	blanks ,,	6⅖	Thirty-two	,,	,,

TABLE No. 4.

When all—   The unplayed dominoes average—

Sixes, fives and fours are out	3
Sixes, fives, fours and threes are out	2
Sixes, fives, fours, threes and twos are out	1

TABLE No. 5.

When all—   The unplayed dominoes average—

Blanks and ones are out	8
Blanks, ones and twos are out	9
Blanks, ones, two and threes are out	10
Blanks, ones, twos, threes and fours are out	11
Blanks, ones, twos, threes, fours and fives, are out	12

Method of finding when it is safe to block the Game.

Suppose all the sixes and fives are played; by the above tables you will know each card must average four.

First see what is the average of pips on all cards played other than the sixes and fives. Suppose they average four.

Now if your cards average *four or more pips less than the average* four, and you have the same or a smaller number of cards than your adversary, to block is a certain win.

For instance, nineteen dominoes are out, all the sixes and fives, and the other six average four. Then, if you have a card (averaging four) to block with and the cards in your hand are the same as those of your adversary and average four less than twelve, you may safely block. Let us prove this :—

The sixes and fives contain 108 pips (page 6).
The other seven cards contain 28 pips.
And your hand of three cards contain 8 pips, 144 in all.

The stock and the adversary's cards must be twenty-four, and if the stock contains the two highest possible, namely double-four and four-three, making fifteen, which is the most disadvantageous it can possibly be for you, you win, as your adversary must have the remaining nine. If the pips on both, or even one of the cards in the stock, are known to you, the calculation will be rendered all the easier.

Sometimes it is quite evident you should block, *e.g.* if you know your adversary holds the double-four and two other cards, which must count one or more, you may safely block, if your pips come to eight.

It is advisable, if there is any chance of your being able to block, to make the calculation in anticipation unbeknown to your antagonist, otherwise if he is a good player he will decide, if you count and refuse to block, to do so himself.

Methods of finding what cards are left in Stock.

1. When your opponent passes a card you can tell from the number you have of that suit in your hand whether there are any in the stock.

2. If during the course of the game you have given your opponent a chance of playing a certain double, and he has refrained from taking advantage of the opportunity, you may safely assume it is in the stock.

A PROBLEM.

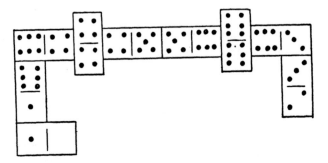

Suppose the game is, as in the diagram, B holds double-three, five-three and five-one, and consequently has to draw, and draws six-two. Ought B to continue to draw? The only inference to be drawn from the play is that sixes is A's strong suit.

B should draw, because if six-blank is in A's hand, B will suffer a disastrous defeat.

Suppose on the other hand that B continues to draw and secures double-blank, he should play it and cease drawing, in hopes that A may foolishly play blank-six, in which case B can block with six-two and win a fine game.

TACTICS OF THE DRAW GAME.

1. A player ought to lead originally from his longest suit ; as if he leads a high double of a suit of which he has no more, or even one indifferent card, he may only be playing his opponent's game.

2. The second player should not, under any circumstances, draw more than half the stock, unless compelled to do so, as by this means he will leave a chance of his opponent drawing an equal number.

3. A good player may at times be justified in taking more than half or even the whole of the stock, as the information obtained by so doing may enable him to play them all before his opponent can play his small number of dominoes.

4. Should the second player hold a good hand, that is one containing a strong suit, consisting of at least three cards of one denomination, and no double unguarded, or a hand comprising dominoes of each suit, he should not draw unless compelled.

5. A player having once commenced to draw, should continue to do so, if he happens to draw a high double, until he holds several of that suit.

6. The player who holds the greater number of dominoes is under a disadvantage ; but on the other hand he very frequently has the compensating advantage of being able to keep both ends open to himself and closed to the adversary, and may by this means run out.

7. In order to win the game, when holding more dominoes than an adversary, after the stock has been exhausted, that

c

is when two cards only remain in it, it is extremely essential to know what it contains.

8. Be careful you do not play into your adversary's hand. Suppose he has shown that twos are his suit (of which you have none), and six-two, five-two, one-two and blank-two are out, you should avoid at all hazards, especially if the stock is full, to play, either a four or a three, as should the adversary hold four-two or three-two, the result might be particularly disastrous.

9. Sometimes it is as well to risk a little to test the nature of the hand against you, in preference to groping in the dark all through the game.

10. You can mostly tell, by looking at your own cards, whether your adversary's are heavy, middling, or light; if your own do not average anything like six, his will be heavy; if yours are about the average, so will his be; and if yours are heavy, his on the other hand will be light.

11. Never hesitate, as a moment's hesitation may give your adversary a hint of something you particularly want to keep from him.

12. Form as clear a notion as possible under the circumstances of your adversary's hand, and then decide whether it is better to run out, block the game, or oblige your adversary to enable you to make Domino.

13. If your antagonist has drawn a large portion of the stock, and has a full hand, while you have very few, if you can contrive to play once or twice, without being blocked, you ought to be pretty sure of winning, because by that time your hand will be so disproportionately small compared with your opponent's, that he will have much difficulty in preventing your winning, without blocking himself.

14. If you have a high hand and there are several cards still in the stock, be careful how you play the fifth of a suit of which you have no more and the double is not out. For instance, suppose six-five, six-two, six-one, six-blank have been played, be careful how you play four-six, as if your adversary has double-six, it will give him an opportunity of playing it, or if he has six-three he may play it to your six, and should you draw the double-six, it will be blocked.

15. If the average of your pips is high, considering the nature of the game, be careful of running any risks. Play a simple game, *i.e.* keep both ends of the game open.

16. It should be always remembered that your antagonist frequently may be in doubt as to the advisability of blocking the game, and often a careless card on your part may afford him just the information he wants.

17. Endeavour to bring these rules to bear, reserving to your discretion as to whether you should in anywise depart from them or use such modifications as the contingencies of the moment may require.

DOMINO DRAW POOL.

This is a decided improvement on Domino Pool. The rules are as in that game, except that if a player cannot match, he is obliged to draw one card from the " stock," when if still unable to match, he says, " Go." Two cards must be left in the " stock " as in other Draw Games.

THE MATADORE GAME.

THIS variety evidently had its birthplace in the land of bull-fights, and is derived from the Spanish word " matar," to kill. It is held by experts to be second only to the Draw Game, and it certainly requires an immense amount of skill to play the matadores and blanks really well. It is the only game of Dominoes which attempts to introduce an equivalent for Trumps. Matadores are, however, more powerful even than trumps, in that they not only over-ride any other card (not a matadore), but can be played at any time, and either end may be placed outside.

The strength of the matadores, or killing dominoes, is in our opinion almost a blot on the game, as between equal players three matadores will almost invariably win against one. It is, however, an exceedingly interesting variation, and affords scope for more diversity of situations, as well as requiring more skill in the manipulation of the cards, than in any other variety.

The cards having been shuffled, each player takes at random seven cards (four is sometimes the number chosen), and the remainder form the talon or stock. The lead may be decided in the usual way, and we recommend that it should be so decided, although we are aware that the method generally adopted is the third one (see page 8).

After the first deal the lead is held alternately by each player, but is drawn for afresh for each new game.

The second player has now to play a card, containing the complement of seven with that on the square at either end of the card already "posed," *i.e.* he must play a one to a six, a two to a five, a four to a three, and *vice versâ*. In play, doubles are considered to be of the value of the pips at one end, not at both.

No card in the "Double Sixes" can possibly contain at one end the complement of seven with a blank, and consequently a matadore has to be played.

Matadores are those dominoes which in themselves bear on their face seven pips or the double-blank. In the ordinary double-six set there are four, namely :—

1. Double-blank. 2. Four-three. 3. Five-two. 4. Six-one.

In addition to being used as a reply to a blank, matadores may be played at any time, quite irrespective of the previous cards played, and may be placed either end outward at the option of the player.

The following diagram shows the method of play :—

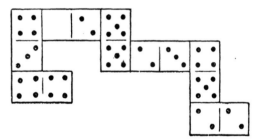

. Suppose the leader plays double-five, you can only pose a domino having two pips at one end, as two-blank, two-one, two-three, two-four, or two-six. Suppose you play two-three, your adversary will have to pose either a four or a two according to the end he may choose, and so on, each player matching, *i.e.* making the adjacent numbers up to seven, or playing a matadore each time his turn comes round. It will be noticed that in the case of the four-three (above) being a matadore, the four end of it is placed adjacent to a blank ; the three might equally have been played, had the player so willed it. A domino, not being a matadore, can only be played when it matches the end of one of the dominoes previously posed.

The second player, if unable to play a matadore or match, *must* draw until able to play, or until the stock is exhausted.

The player who draws an unplayable card from the stock, of course retains it in his hand.

On the other hand, the second and each succeeding player, even though able to match, or pose a matadore, or both, is at liberty to draw from the stock, provided he leaves two dominoes.

When the stock is exhausted, a player unable to match, and not having a matadore, says " go;" and his opponent is bound to proceed, if possible. To call " go " only forfeits the turn ; and the player calling it is allowed, in fact, *must*, play when his turn comes round again, if he can.

The game proceeds in this manner until one player has played all his dominoes, or there is a "block," *i.e.*, when neither can play, and all the stock is exhausted except two.

The game is usually one hundred up, and three games make up a rubber ; but any other number of points can be fixed on by agreement between the players.

It sometimes happens that one player scores a hundred without his opponent scoring at all ; this is called a Zapatero, and counts as two games.

The scoring is as in the Draw game, only the adversary's pips are counted in the case of a block, and not the sum of all the dominoes unplayed. Doubles count all the pips at both ends, not, as in play, those at either end.

This game is seen at its best when played by two persons, but it can be played by three players, with the ordinary pack ; if more wish to play, dominoes ranging up to double-nines, or even to double-twelves, should be used.

When three play, the one who has the lowest number of pips scores the number of pips held by the player who has most, and not the sum of the pips held by his opponents.

When four play, they should cut for partners, and play as at Whist. The two partners, whose total number of pips is lower than that of their opponents, score the sum of their opponents' pips.

If a set of double-nines is used, the method of play is unchanged, except that the number to be made each time is ten. Thus, if a domino is played, say seven-eight, it must be matched at the seven end by a three, and at the eight end by a two, and the matadores are nine-one, eight-two, seven-three, six-four, double-fives, and double-blank, the dominoes in the whole pack being fifty-five.

Likewise, if the double-twelve pack is used, the number to be made each time is thirteen, and the matadores are, twelve-one, eleven-two, ten-three, nine-four, eight-five, seven-six, and double-blank, the dominoes in the whole pack being ninety-one.

TACTICS OF THE MATADORE GAME.

1. In the first lead off, if you happen to hold double-blank, and one or two of the other matadores, you should lead the double-blank, which will probably oblige your opponent to draw a good portion of the stock.

2. If the double-blank, or any single matadore is dealt you, avoid playing it until necessary. Matadores, for the most part, are to be hoarded up, as they are valuable to prevent your having to draw at a critical stage of the game, when there is a blank at both ends.

3. It is advisable to lead off with a double, even in pre-

ference to getting rid of a high card, as it leaves your opponent no choice as to his play.

4. If blanks have been played at both ends, and you hold double-blank, play it, as it shifts the responsibility of drawing on to your adversary's shoulders, or forces a matadore.

5. When drawing, do not be too hasty in playing a matadore, should you be lucky enough to obtain one, but use your judgment as to whether you ought to continue to draw or not.

6. Matadores are especially valuable, as a player will soon find, but are far more formidable for defensive than offensive purposes, *i.e.* they are able at all times to save your drawing probably a great many of the stock ; but to attack your adversary they are not, if we except the double-blank, any more powerful than ordinary cards.

7. Matadores should not be played, and you should draw rather than play one, if your adversary can possibly hold the cards that will block you again. For instance, suppose you play four-three when there is a blank at both ends, and you do not hold either blank-four or blank-three, you run the risk of being blocked again, if your adversary holds either or both. If you hold one of them, say the three-blank, you can play the matadore, placing the four outside.

If you hold neither, it will be wiser to draw (if there are several cards in the stock) until you obtain one of them, as then you can play your matadore with comparative safety.

8. A score is obtained by the player who has fewer pips at the end of the game, consequently you should draw sparingly, using your judgment as to whether the cards and the information you are likely to get is worth the risk of drawing several.

9. Never play a blank unless you have a matadore, or one end is already blocked. If your adversary goes out of his way to play a blank, it shows that he holds matadores; so, never under such circumstances, play a blank unless you have two matadores, as you will be playing into his hand.

10. A player should pay especial attention to the blanks which guard any matadore (not the double-blank) which he may hold, as should such matadore guard be in the adversary's hand, the matadore is to a very great extent neutralized.

Matadore six-one   is guarded by six-blank, one-blank.
   „   five-two   „   „   „ five-blank, two-blank.
   „   four-three „   „   „ four-blank, three-blank.

10. To illustrate this point, suppose A holds two matadores, three-four and five-two, and five other cards; his hand might not prove effective if B held double-blank and the four guarding blanks. B should keep the guards or "picadors," and should draw moderately, rather than part with them.

When once the matadore is played, B should block the end, and use the other blank as soon as possible.

11. Never "pose" a blank unless you have at least two matadores.

12. A mixed hand, *i.e.* one containing cards of each suit, is a good playable one, and unless the opponent has overwhelming strength in matadores, is likely to score.

13. A long suit is also valuable, but three of two suits which are complementary is still more effective, either sixes and ones, fives and twos, or fours and threes.

Suppose you hold three sixes and three ones, play the sixes, thereby forcing your adversary's ones, or compelling him to draw or sacrifice a matadore.

14. When your adversary declares strength by playing blanks, and you do not hold the double-blank, especially refrain from playing any card of which he may hold the blank. This you may do by playing the complement of the blanks already down.

15. Blanks are very valuable, the double-blank especially so. If you hold a long suit of blanks, together with the double, it is often good play to block the game at every opportunity, and exhaust your opponent's matadores.

16. If there is any reason to suppose that the blanks are held by your adversary, prevent him from using them as much as possible.

If you do not hold six-blank, four-blank, or two-blank, avoid playing a one, three, or five, not, however, to such an extent as may injure your hand, but when in doubt between two cards choose one in preference which is not a one, three, or five.

There is a variation of the Matadore game in which a matadore, when played, scores one, and one is also scored for every seven or multiple of seven that appears jointly at the opposite ends of the game. Doubles counting their full number of pips. Thus a double-six and a double-one, making fourteen, would score two towards game.

This variation is not to be recommended, as it further complicates a difficult game, and is evidently an attempt to assimilate it to all fives and all threes.

THE BERGEN GAME.

THE lead is drawn for, and the cards are shuffled in the usual way. Each player then takes six cards.

The game is generally one-hundred up, and for two persons.

If a double is first posed, the player makes a " double header," for which he scores twenty points. In play also, when both ends of the game are made the same, the player so making them also scores a " double header."

Thus, if A poses one-six, B plays six-three; should A play three-one, making both ends ones or threes, he thereby is entitled to score a double header.

Now, if B plays a double-three, if both ends are three already, he makes a " triple header," which scores thirty.

A player must play if able to match, and if unable, *must* draw one card from the stock; and if still unable to play, cries " Go," when his opponent plays or draws one card, and so on, each playing alternately, until all except two dominoes have been drawn from the stock, or until one player makes " domino," for which he scores ten points.

When all the stock except two are drawn, and neither player can match, it is a block, and the holder of the smaller number of doubles wins, and scores ten points.

If both players hold the same number of doubles, the hand which contains the lowest double wins, and scores ten.

For instance : A holds double-six and double-blank, and B double-two and double-one. A wins.

If neither player holds a double, the hand which contains the smaller number of pips wins, and scores ten.

Neither a triple nor double header alone is able to win the game.

If a player makes a double or triple header when at 90, he scores nothing ; if at 80, he scores ten points, for either a double or triple header ; if at 70, he scores 20 points for either.

Should three players wish to play, the rules are the same as in the Two game ; but if four persons play, there is no drawing, and the remaining four cards form the reserve.

DOMINO LOO.

CARD-BOARD dominoes are far better for this game than the bone or ivory ones, and if used, should be cut, shuffled, and dealt like playing cards.

When only two persons play, the one who cuts the higher card deals, and his opponent has the lead.

Afterwards the lead is alternate throughout the game.

In cutting, doubles count before any ordinary card, thus if A cuts double-blank and B six-five, A deals.

Each player has five cards dealt to him, and the dealer turns up the trump-card. Unless a double is turned up, the higher end of the turned-up card is the trump suit.

If a player is not satisfied with his hand, he may take " miss," *i.e.* throw away his cards and take six others from the top of the pack, and after examination must discard one of them. The dealer may exchange one of his cards for the turn-up, or may take miss, but he must not do both.

The method of play is unlike that of all other Domino games, the players proceeding as in Loo.

The leader plays a card and his opponent plays to it, as in that game. The two cards so played, make up a trick, and the winner of the trick has the next lead. The higher card of the suit led, not necessarily the higher domino, wins the trick. Any card led, other than a double or a trump, may be one of two suits, according to the pleasure of the leader. Thus if five-one is led, the holder of it may call five-one or one-five ; in the former case, any five other than the five-blank would beat it, but in the latter only a one-six, double-one, or a trump would do so.

The value of the cards is as follows : the double of the trump suit is the highest ; then rank the rest of the trump suit in their numerical order, a six ranking higher than a five, and so on ; then the rest of the plain suits. The cards in plain suits rank as follows : the double, the six, five, four, etc.

The double is the highest card in each suit, double-blank ranking before blank-six.

The leader of each case must announce which is the suit he desires the card to be. If he plays four-blank, and calls it thus : four is the suit, but if he calls blank-four, blank is the suit. He should also announce a trump when led, although in this case he has no option.

The rules of play are as in Loo ; if you hold two trumps, lead one, and play a trump after winning a trick, if possible. Also follow suit, when able. No player is bound to head, or win the trick, if he can play otherwise, according to rule ; but if he renounces a suit, he must trump if he can.

It is sometimes the rule to loo a player who breaks any of these rules, and make him pay the extra penalty of not scoring during that hand. This is too severe, and to forfeit one or two points for the error committed, is far more just.

Each trick counts one, and the game is fifteen up.

A player who does not take a trick is looed, *i.e.* loses five points, and if he is nothing up, he is made to owe five ; in other words, he will want twenty points to win the game.

Domino Loo can also be played by three or four players. If three play, there are only two misses of six cards each ; but when four play, there is only one miss of seven cards two of which are discarded after being looked at by the player.

The deal goes round in succession to the left, and the players play in order, the one on the left of the dealer playing first, and so on.

The best way of scoring when more than two play, is to form a pool, each contributing a stake which is divisible by five, except the dealer, who contributes a double stake.

Each hand, then, is a game in itself, and the winner of each trick is entitled to a fifth of the pool. The rules of play are the same as in the game for two ; but here, if any player breaks any of the ordinary rules, he should be looed. If any player is looed, he contributes to the next pool as much as there was in the previous one.

This contribution is sometimes unlimited, but it is advisable to limit the amount of a loo to four times the original stake, when three play, and to five times the original stake when four play.

When there is a loo, no player not looed, contributes to the pool, except the dealer, who puts in the original stake.

When this game is played with a pool, no player is bound to play, and may pass ; in which case he loses his chance of the pool, but cannot be looed.

Any player, however, who takes miss, must play.

If all pass but one, and the dealer is desirous of doing so too, he can, if he pleases, take miss ; or if no miss remains, can play his own hand for the benefit of the pool, *i.e.* any share of the pool he may win is left in towards the next pool, and he cannot be looed. He must, however, make a distinct declaration that he is not playing for himself, otherwise the presumption will be that he is doing so. If all pass except the dealer, he takes the pool.

Before closing our remarks on the subject of Dominoes we think it necessary to make an observation or two on the etiquette of the game. No talking about the game, or hints of what cards any player may hold, should be permitted for an instant, as any such proceeding is quite unjustifiable. It proceeds, we are quite aware, more from thoughtlessness than anything else, but when it is pointed out it should be rigidly avoided by every right-thinking person.

Such remarks as "Oh, well, I cannot possibly run out now," just after the last ordinary six has been played, is equivalent to saying, "I hold the 'double-six.'"

Or again, "You cannot block me this time," addressed to one's predecessor, would convey that the speaker holds one of each suit at the two ends of the game.

If the remark only injured the offender in this matter, it would be of little consequence, and for this reason it is not so much to be deprecated in the games between two players, but in games for four or more, such remarks may help one player, and seriously injure the rest.

Domino players are by no means the only offenders in this respect, a fact patent to any casual visitor who may chance to stroll into the card room of any club, whether in London or the provinces.

Rules of the Game.

1. Each player shall be entitled to shuffle the cards before the play commences.

2. If it is found that one of the players has drawn more than the number of dominoes agreed upon, his opponent may withdraw the extra number, and put it or them back into the stock or reserve, keeping the withdrawn card or cards face downwards.

3. Should the player in error have seen the card or cards, his opponent shall have the right of doing so as well.

4. If any player take into his hand, or even see one of the two cards that should be left in the stock, it shall be replaced in the stock, and the adversary be also entitled to look at it.

5. If any card is turned, by accident, face uppermost on the table, it may be retaken into the player's hand, and no penalty shall be exacted, as his adversary has gained the information where the card is.

6. Should a player expose a card deliberately in the act of playing, he shall be obliged to play it at one or other of the ends of the game if he can legally do so.

7. No player shall be allowed to take back into his hand, or alter the position of any card when once it has been played and quitted, *i.e.* when it is laid on the table, touching the dominoes already played, and no longer in contact with the player's hand.

SOLITAIRE.

IT is not improbable that this popular game was originally suggested by the foreign game "German Tactics." For although the movements are different, the thirty-three positions on both the boards are arranged alike. Or it may be an ancient French game remodelled, in which marbles are used instead of pegs and the number of points are thirty-three instead of thirty-seven.

By a French authority who wrote at the beginning of this century, Solitaire is thus defined, "Sorte de jeu qui se joue au moyen d'une petite table percée de trente-sept trous et avec trente-six chevilles."

If Solitaire does not require the profound skill necessary to play Chess, the player is never wearied by a protracted game. If it does not call into exercise all the moral qualities required by Chess, yet it may fairly lay claim to three of them—namely, foresight, circumspection, and caution.

Solitaire is generally played on a circular wooden board, having holes arranged in the form shown in the diagram. At the beginning of the game all the holes are filled with glass marbles, then one marble is taken out of its hole and placed on one side.

The method of proceeding then is to make any marble hop over any other where there is a vacant space immediately beyond, the one which is hopped over being removed from the board. The moves are made vertically or horizontally in either direction, but never diagonally.

A3	A4	A5		
B3	B4	B5		
C1	C2	C3	C4	C5	C6	C7
D1	D2	D3	D4	D5	D6	D7
E1	E2	E3	E4	E5	E6	E7
		F3	F4	F5	
		G3	G4	G5	

DIAGRAM OF SOLITAIRE BOARD.

For instance, Suppose D4 is removed, then B4, D2, F4, or D6 is allowed to hop over and remove C4, D3, E4, or D5, as the case may be, and deposit itself in D4.

The object of the game is to take off all the balls but one.

Some writers on this game have shown how it is possible to take off the ball in any hole on the board and leave a ball at the conclusion in the same hole, giving 33 different solutions to point this out.

This is wholly unnecessary in our opinion, for the following reasons. If it is shown how to take off A3, this will also give a solution for C7, G5, and E1, as if the board is turned a quarter round from left to right A3 becomes C7, if half-way round it becomes G5 and three-quarters round E1.

D

A4 in like manner becomes D7, G4, D1. As one arm of a Greek cross is the same as another, it is obvious at a glance—that there can only be ten different games under the conditions viz., A3, A4, A5, B3, B4, B5, C3, C4, C5, D4. But C3 becomes C5 if the board is turned a quarter round, consequently C5 may be also eliminated.

Although A3 and B3 are very similar to A5 and B5 respectively, it is necessary to give a solution for

A3, A4, A5, B3, B4, B5, C3, C4, and D4.

How to solve A3, C7, G5, E1.

Move.		Move.	
1.	C3 to A3.	9.	G3 to E3.
2.	C1 to C3.	10.	D3 to F3.
3.	C4 to C2.	11.	G5 to G3 on to E3.
4.	C6 to C4.	12.	F5 to F3 on to D3.
5.	E5 to C5, C3.	13.	C3 to E3.
6.	E7 to E5.	14.	A5 to C5.
7.	E4 to E6.	15.	C7 to E7 on to E5.
8.	E2 to E4.	16.	E1 to C1 on to C3.

Move.
17. A3 to A5.
18. E4 to E2 on to C2, C4, C6, E6, E4, C4, A4.
19. A5 to A3.

How to solve A4, D1, D7, G4.

Move.		Move.	
1.	C4 to A4.	10.	E5 to C5.
2.	C2 to C4.	11.	E7 to E5.
3.	D4 to B4.	12.	G4 to E4 on to E6.
4.	A3 to C3.	13.	B5 to D5.
5.	D3 to B3.	14.	G5 to E5 on to C5.
6.	F3 to D3.	15.	C1 to E1 on to E3.
7.	E1 to E3.	16.	D3 to F3.
8.	E4 to E2.	17.	G3 to E3.
9.	C6 to C4.	18.	A5 to A3 on to C3.

Move.
19. C7 to E7 on to E5.
20. C4 to C2, E2, E4, E6, C6, C4, A4.

How to solve A_5, C_1, E_7, G_3.

Move.

1. C5 to A5.
2. C7 to C5.
3. C4 to C6.
4. C2 to C4.
5. E3 to C3 on to C5.
6. E1 to E3.
7. E4 to E2.
8. E6 to E4.

Move.

9. G5 to E5.
10. D5 to F5.
11. G3 to G5 on to E5.
12. F3 to F5 on to D5.
13. C5 to E5.
14. E7 to C7 on to C5.
15. C1 to E1 on to E3.
16. A3 to C3.

Move.

17. A5 to A3.
18. E4 to C4, C2, E2, E4, E6, C6, C4, A4.
19. A3 to A5.

How to solve B_3, C_6, F_5, E_2.

Move.

1. D3 to B3.
2. F3 to D3.
3. C5 to C3 on to E3.
4. A5 to C5.
5. D5 to D3 on to F3.
6. F5 to D5 on to B5.
7. C1 to C3.
8. G3 to E3.

Move.

9. D1 to D3 on to F3.
10. C7 to C5.
11. B5 to D5.
12. E7 to E5 on to C5.
13. D7 to D5 on to B5.
14. E1 to E3 on to E5.
15. G5 to G3 on to E3.
16. A3 to A5 on to C5.

Move.

17. B3 to B5, D5, F5, F3, D3, B3.

How to solve B_4, D_2, D_6, F_4.

Move.

1. D4 to B4.
2. D6 to D4.
3. F5 to D5.
4. D4 to D6.
5. F4 to D4.
6. E7 to E5.
7. E2 to E4 on to E6.
8. G3 to E3.
9. D3 to F3.

Move.

10. B3 to D3.
11. C1 to C3.
12. D3 to B3.
13. A3 to C3.
14. C6 to C4 on to C2.
15. A5 to C5.
16. C7 to E7 on to E5.
17. E1 to C1 on to C3.
18. G5 to G3 on to E3.

Move.

19. A4 to C4, C2, E2, E4, E6, C6, C4.
20. D4 to B4.

How to solve B5, E6, F3, C2.

Move.   Move.

1. D5 to B5.
2. F5 to D5.
3. C3 to C5 on to E5.
4. A3 to C3.
5. D3 to D5 on to F5.
6. F3 to D3 on to B3.
7. C7 to C5.
8. G5 to E5.

9. D7 to D5 on to F5.
10. C1 to C3.
11. B3 to D3.
12. E1 to E3 on to C3.
13. D1 to D3 on to B3.
14. E7 to E5 on to E3.
15. G3 to G5 on to E5.
16. A5 to A3 on to C3.

Move.

17. B5 to D5, F5, F3, D3, B3, B5.

How to solve C3, C5, E3, E5.

Move.   Move.

1. C1 to C3.
2. C4 to C2.
3. E4 to C4.
4. E2 to E4.
5. E5 to E3.
6. G4 to E4 on to E2.
7. E7 to E5.
8. G3 to E3.

9. E2 to E4 on to E6.
10. A3 to C3 on to E3.
11. C5 to C3.
12. G5 to E5 on to C5.
13. C6 to C4.
14. C3 to C5.
15. C7 to E7 on to E5.
16. E1 to C1 on to C3.

Move.

17. A4 to C4, C2, E2, E4, E6, C6, C4.
18. A5 to C5, C3.

How to solve C4, D3, D5, E4.

Move.   Move.

1. C6 to C4.
2. C3 to C5.
3. A3 to C3.
4. C2 to C4 on to C6.
5. C7 to C5.
6. E4 to C4 on to C6.
7. E3 to C3.
8. E1 to E3.

9. E6 to E4 on to E2.
10. G5 to E5.
11. D5 to F5.
12. G3 to G5 on to E5.
13. F3 to F5 on to D5.
14. A5 to C5 on to E5.
15. C1 to E1 on to E3.
16. E7 to C7 on to C5.

Move.

17. A4 to C4, C2, E2, E4, E6, C6, C4.

How to solve D4.

Move.

1.	D6 to D4.	9.	C1 to C3.
2.	D3 to D5.	10.	C4 to C2.
3.	F4 to D4 on to D6.	11.	C6 to C4.
4.	F5 to D5.	12.	A5 to C5.
5.	E7 to E5.	13.	D5 to B5.
6.	E2 to E4 on to E6.	14.	A3 to A5 on to C5.
7.	G3 to E3.	15.	C7 to E7 on to E5.
8.	B3 to D3 on to F3.	16.	E1 to C1 on to C3.

Move.

17. G5 to G3 on to E3.
18. C4 to C2, E2, E4, E6, C6, C4.
19. B4 to D4.

Corollary 1. If D4 is left vacant, it is obvious the last ball can be left on A4 by finishing the eighteenth move at A4, instead of C4.

Corollary 2. If the board is turned a quarter of the way round, D4 can be left vacant, and the last ball left in D7. And, in like manner, the last ball can be left in G4 and D1 by turning the board half-way and three-quarters the way round respectively, and proceeding as in solution of D4.

Corollary 3. D7 can be left vacant, and the last ball left in D4, by making the first move D5 to D7 and the rest the same as in the solution of D4.

Corollary 4. D7 can be left vacant and the last ball left in A4, by making first move D5 to D7, second to seventeenth, as given above, and eighteenth C4 to C2, E2, E4, E6, C6, C4 and on to A4.

It will be found that a ball may be taken out of either of five holes, A4, D1, D7, G4 and D4, and the last ball left in any one of them.

Our readers must be warned against taking a ball from any other hole except the five above-mentioned, and at- tempting to leave the last ball in the centre hole.

Many other pretty Solitaire problems might be pointed out did the limits of this article permit; but any one who has followed us thus far will probably be able to set them to himself.

DIAGRAM OF OLD FRENCH BOARD.

The old French board on which the game used to be played was of octagonal form, and contained thirty-seven holes. It has been superseded to a very great extent by the new board already described, owing, doubtless, to the difficulty of many of its problems. This board being more difficult, has some advantages over its later rival; and players of Solitaire are recommended to try it and some of its problems, of which we now give a few specimens.

PROBLEM I.

THE CORSAIR.

Take off No. 1, and leave a ball at 37.

Move.		Move.		Move.		Move.	
1.	11 to 1.	7.	9 to 11.	13.	36 to 26.	19.	22 to 20.
2.	9 to 11.	8.	18 to 5.	14.	3 to 13.	20.	27 to 13.
3.	24 to 10.	9.	1 to 11.	15.	13 to 27.	21.	29 to 27.
4.	4 to 17.	10.	14 to 12.	16.	15 to 13.	22.	26 to 28.
5.	12 to 10.	11.	28 to 14.	17.	12 to 14.	23.	34 to 21.
6.	23 to 9.	12.	26 to 28.	18.	8 to 21.	24.	37 to 27.
				25.	30 to 32,		

which leaves eleven balls on the board—namely, 2, 6, 11, 13, 17, 19, 21, 25, 27, 32, and 35.

Move.
26. 2 to 12, on to 26, 24, 10, 12, 14, 28, 26, 36.
27. 35 to 37.

PROBLEM II.

LE LECTEUR AU MILIEU DE SES AMIS.

Take off a ball at 19, and leave the central ball surrounded by sixteen balls.

Move.		Move.		
1.	6 to 19.	11.	33 to 31.	*Leaving the board thus:*
2.	4 to 6.	12.	27 to 25.	
3.	18 to 5.	13.	25 to 35.	
4.	6 to 4.	14.	29 to 27.	
5.	9 to 11.	15.	14 to 28.	
6.	24 to 10.	16.	27 to 29.	
7.	11 to 9.	17.	19 to 21.	
8.	26 to 24.	18.	7 to 20.	
9.	35 to 25.	19.	21 to 19.	
10.	24 to 26.			

PROBLEM III.

Take off a ball at 19, and leave five balls in a central cross.

Move.		Move.		
1.	6 to 19.	17.	18 to 5.	
2.	8 to 6.	18.	5 to 7.	
3.	2 to 12.	19.	7 to 20.	*Leaving the board thus:*
4.	4 to 6.	20.	20 to 18.	
5.	18 to 5.	21.	17 to 19.	
6.	20 to 7.	22.	23 to 25.	
7.	1 to 11.	23.	36 to 26.	
8.	3 to 13.	24.	26 to 24.	
9.	16 to 18.	25.	35 to 25.	
10.	22 to 20.	26.	24 to 26.	
11.	30 to 17.	27.	29 to 27.	
12.	34 to 21.	28.	27 to 25.	
13.	26 to 24.	29.	9 to 11.	
14.	12 to 26.	30.	15 to 13.	
15.	26 to 28.	31.	37 to 27.	
16.	21 to 19.			

Problem IV.

LE TRICOLET.

Take off a ball at 19, and leave a cross of sixteen balls.

Leaving the board thus:

Move.		Move.	
1.	6 to 19.	11.	21 to 19.
2.	10 to 12.	12.	7 to 20.
3.	19 to 6.	13.	19 to 21.
4.	2 to 12.	14.	22 to 20.
5.	4 to 6.	15.	8 to 21.
6.	17 to 19.	16.	32 to 19.
7.	31 to 18.	17.	28 to 26.
8.	19 to 17.	18.	19 to 32.
9.	16 to 18.	19.	36 to 26.
10.	30 to 17.	20.	34 to 32.

Problem V.

Take off 12, and leave a ball in 26.

Move.		Move.		Move.		Move.	
1.	2 to 12.	10.	16 to 18.	19.	30 to 17.	28.	21 to 19.
2.	4 to 6.	11.	18 to 5.	20.	26 to 28.	29.	36 to 26.
3.	12 to 2.	12.	22 to 20.	21.	29 to 27.	30.	26 to 24.
4.	8 to 6.	13.	20 to 7.	22.	12 to 26.	31.	24 to 10.
5.	2 to 12.	14.	9 to 11.	23.	26 to 28.	32.	35 to 25.
6.	18 to 5.	15.	15 to 13.	24.	37 to 27.	33.	25 to 11.
7.	20 to 7.	16.	5 to 18.	25.	28 to 26.	34.	10 to 12.
8.	1 to 11.	17.	7 to 20.	26.	26 to 24.	35.	12 to 26.
9.	3 to 13.	18.	34 to 21.	27.	23 to 25.		

Problem VI.

Take off 6, and leave a ball at 32.

Move.		Move.		Move.		Move.	
1.	19 to 6.	10.	2 to 12.	19.	18 to 31.	28.	36 to 26.
2.	10 to 12.	11.	12 to 10.	20.	35 to 25.	29.	26 to 12.
3.	1 to 11.	12.	17 to 19.	21.	16 to 18.	30.	12 to 14.
4.	12 to 10.	13.	4 to 17.	22.	18 to 31.	31.	29 to 27.
5.	14 to 12.	14.	20 to 18.	23.	30 to 32.	32.	8 to 21.
6.	3 to 13.	15.	32 to 19.	24.	28 to 26.	33.	22 to 20.
7.	12 to 14.	16.	18 to 20.	25.	37 to 27.	34.	20 to 33.
8.	9 to 11.	17.	31 to 18.	26.	26 to 28.	35.	34 to 32.
9.	15 to 13.	18.	23 to 25.	27.	21 to 19.		

CPSIA information can be obtained at www.ICGtesting.com
Printed in the USA
LVOW11s2221030914

402361LV00001B/46/P

9 781406 789621